Gannets

Written by Sandra Iversen

A lot of birds live on this big rock.
The birds are gannets.
It is springtime.

A lot goes on in springtime.
The gannets find a mate.
They make a nest.
Some nests are by the edge
of the rock.

nest on rock edge

The female gannet lays an egg.
She sits on the nest.
The male gannet goes to find fish.
He has to fly off the rock.
He has to dive into the ocean
to find fish.

male gannet finding fish

The male gannet comes back.
He looks down
to see if he can find his mate.
He sees her but he cannot land.
He has to fly by.

When the chicks hatch,
they cannot fly.
One day they will try to fly.
They will fly a long way away.

Some day they will fly back to the rock.